FEDERICO FEDERICI

STUTTGARTER STRUKTURFONIEN

A GNU Octave Symphony

LN
libri della neve

Each document is a unique source of signs to be merged into new alphabet-like traces within a simulated writing.

Dedicated supervised image processing scripts were developed to acquire and plunge sheet music into abstract asemic spaces.

The image matrix is morphologically manipulated with the help of routines, which combine neighbouring clusters of pixels according to certain structuring shapes (line, square, disk, etc.) and depending on specific elements (point, centre, size, etc.) to be adjusted until a new formal equilibrium is attained.

All code segments have been developed, tested and run within Linux GNU Octave. Preliminary image analysis benefited standard ImageJ plug-ins.

```
% fragment
x=imread('im.jpg');
E=2*rand(1);
SE5=strel('arbitrary', E);
V=[2,3];
SE=strel('periodicline', 1, V);
SE1=strel('line', 1, 1);
SE3=strel('square', 1);
NHOOD=[1 0 0 0 0 0 0 0 1 1 1 1 1 0, 1 0 0 0 0 1 0 1 0
1 0 1 1 1 0 1 1 1 1];
SE4=strel(NHOOD);
OFFSET=[10, -18];
SE2=strel('pair', OFFSET);
A=imerode(x, SE1);
A1=imerode(A, SE4);
A2=imerode(A1, SE3);
A3=imerode(A2, SE);
B =imerode(A3, SE5);
imwrite(B, 'imsaved.jpg');
```

5

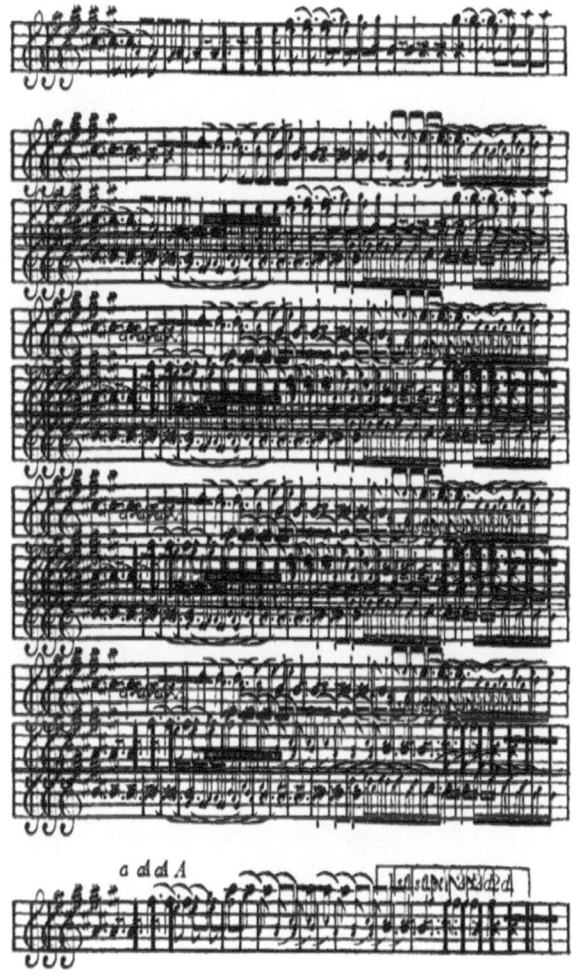

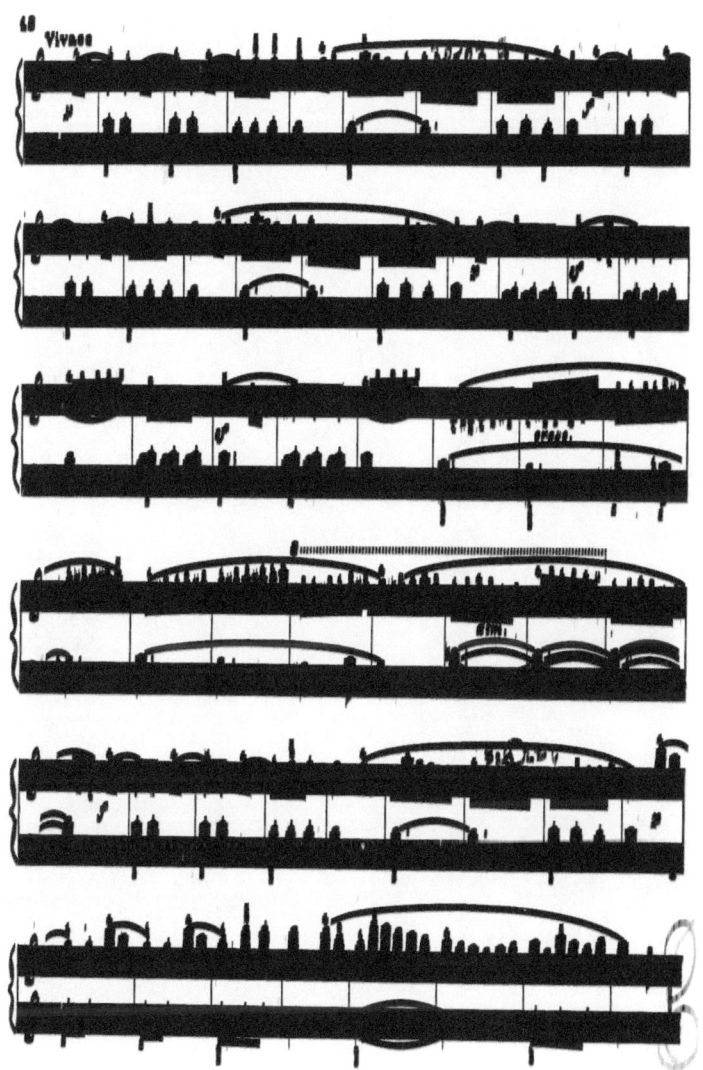

9

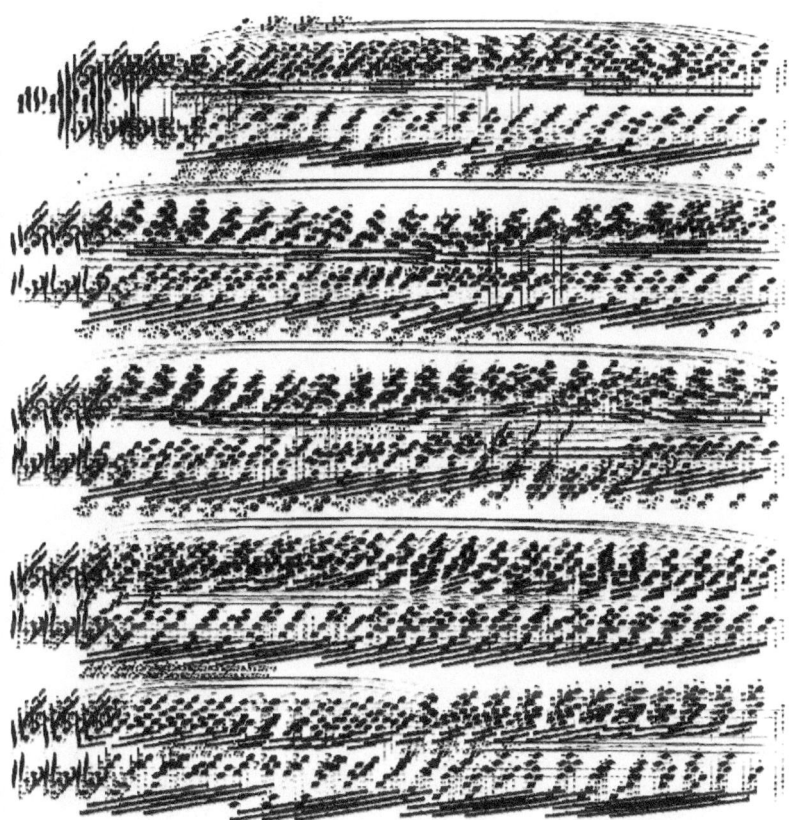

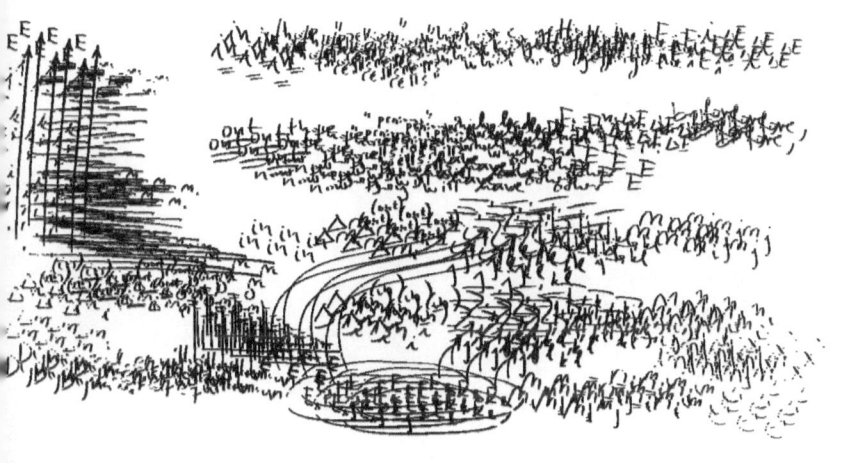

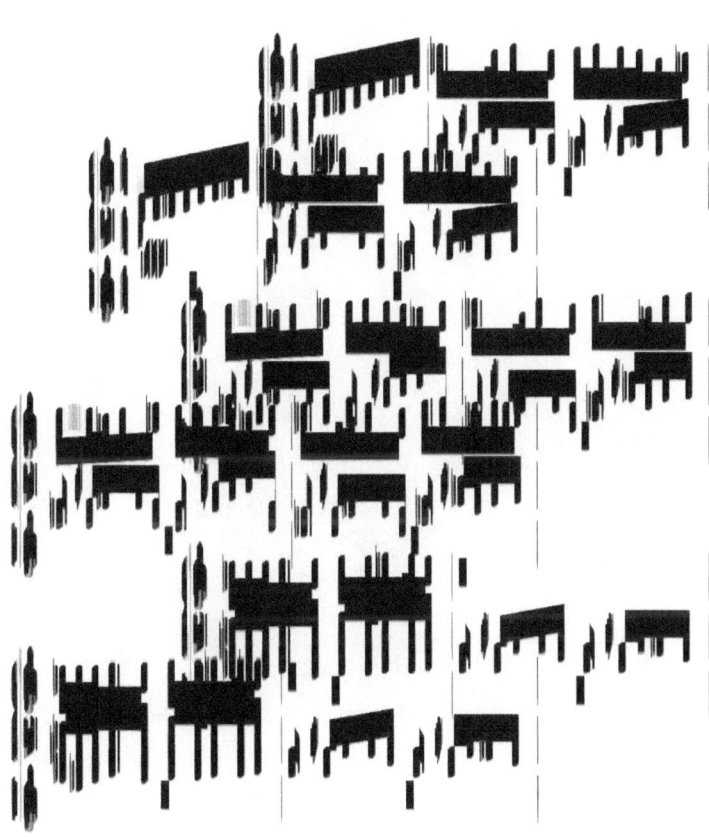

17

25

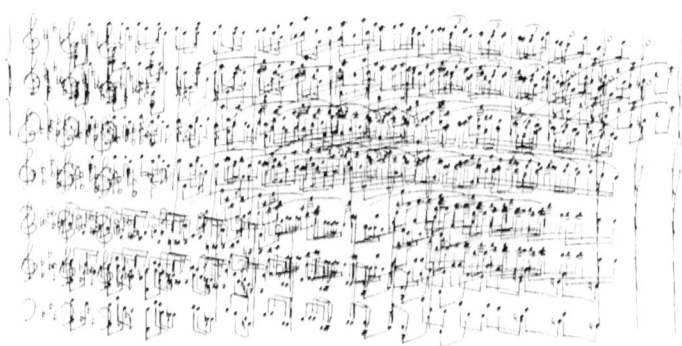

27

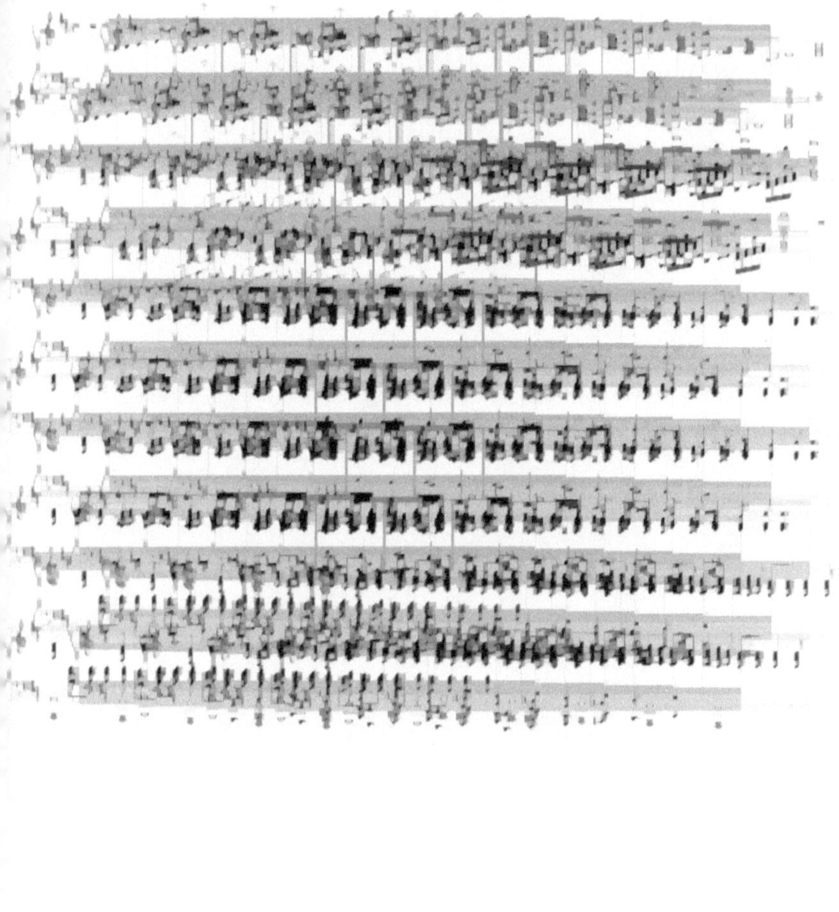

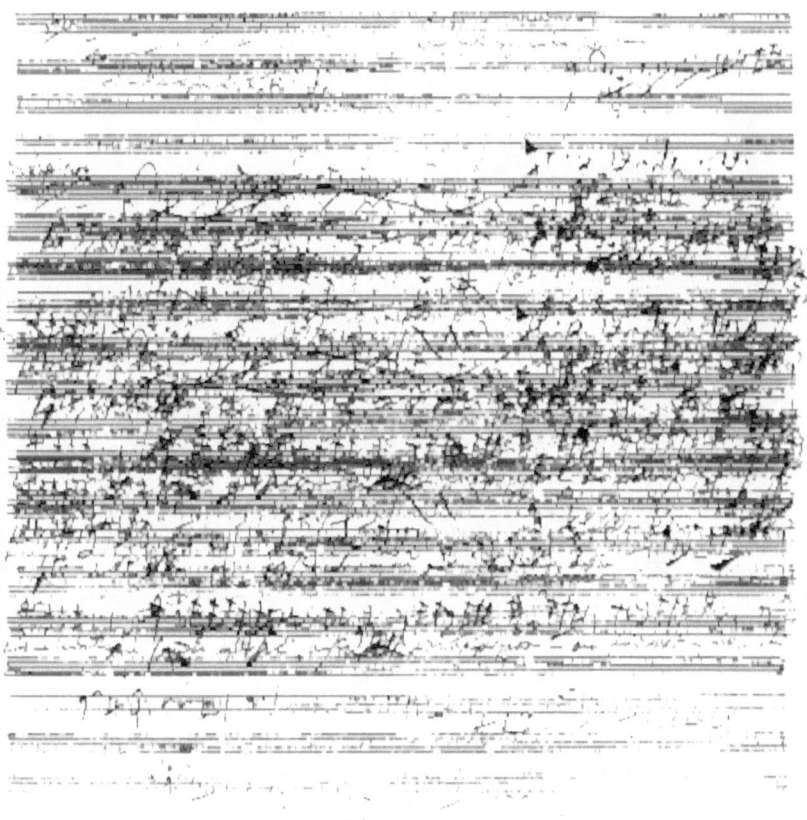

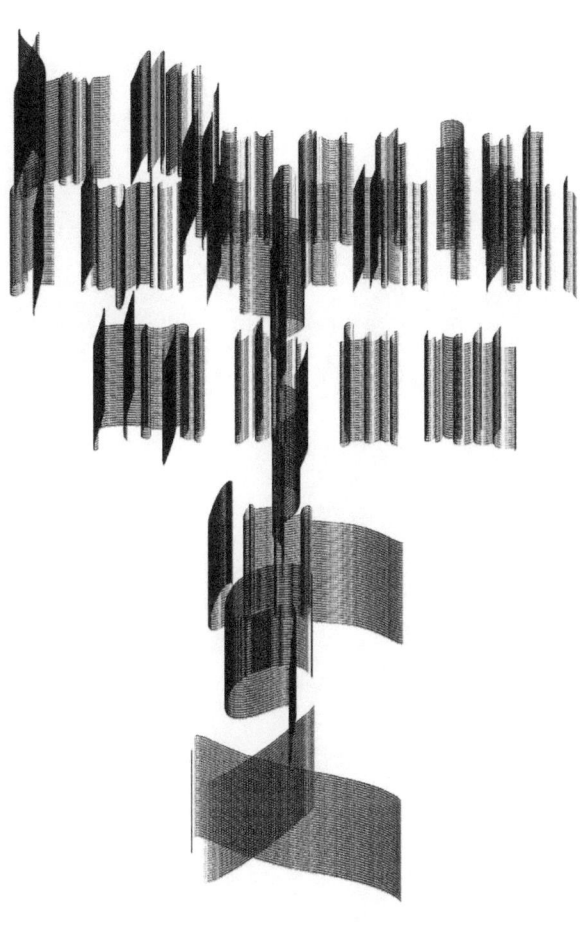

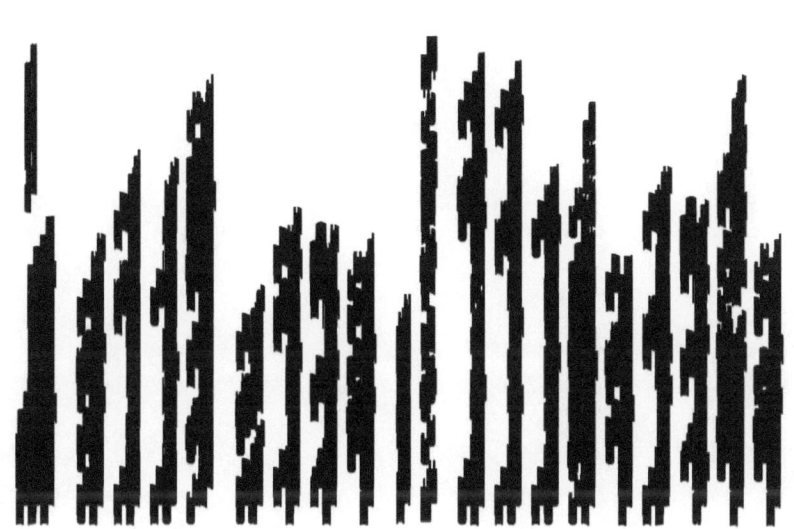

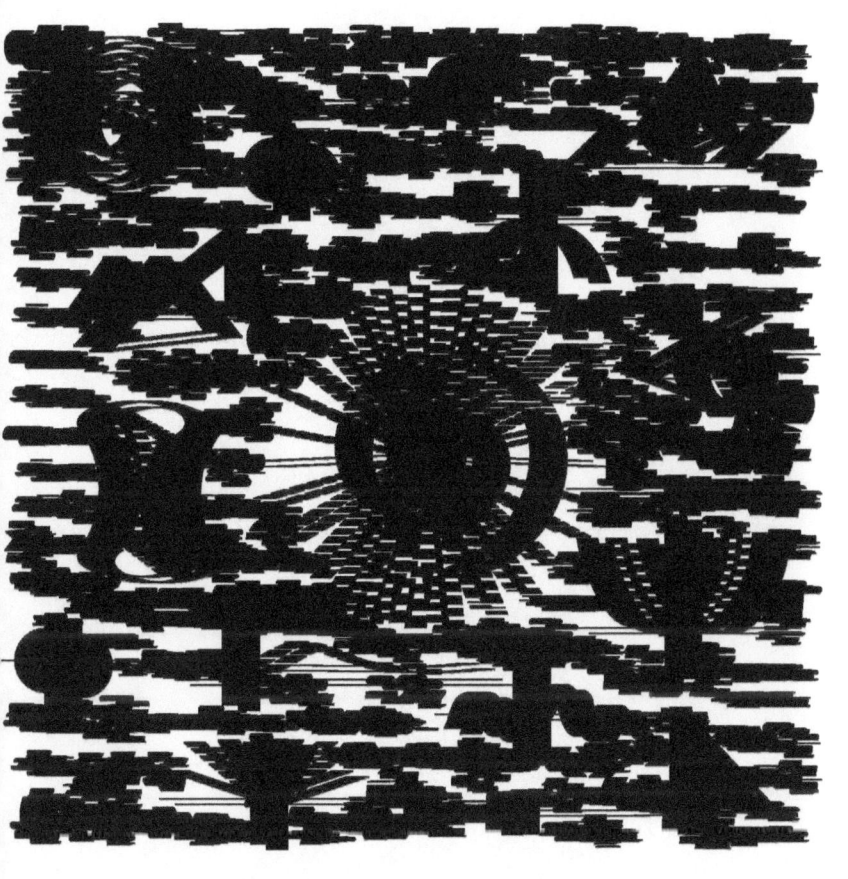

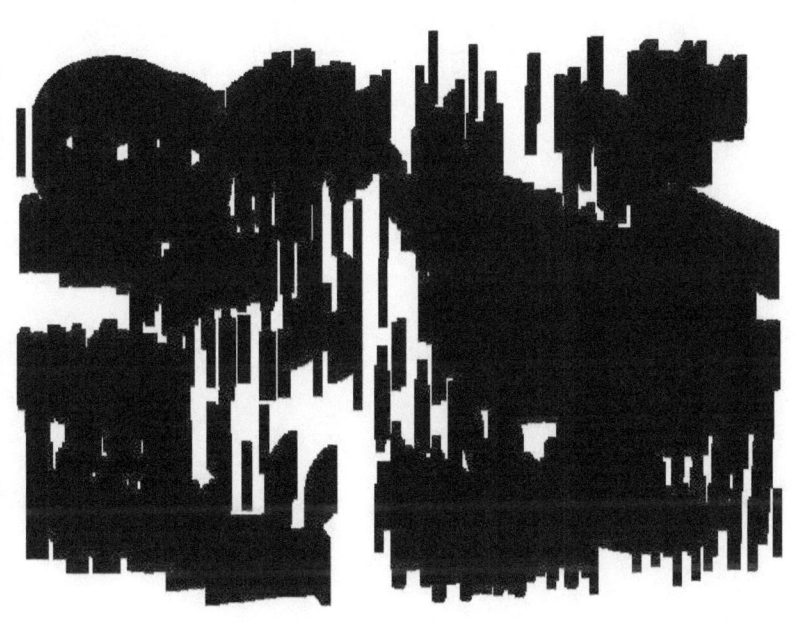

41

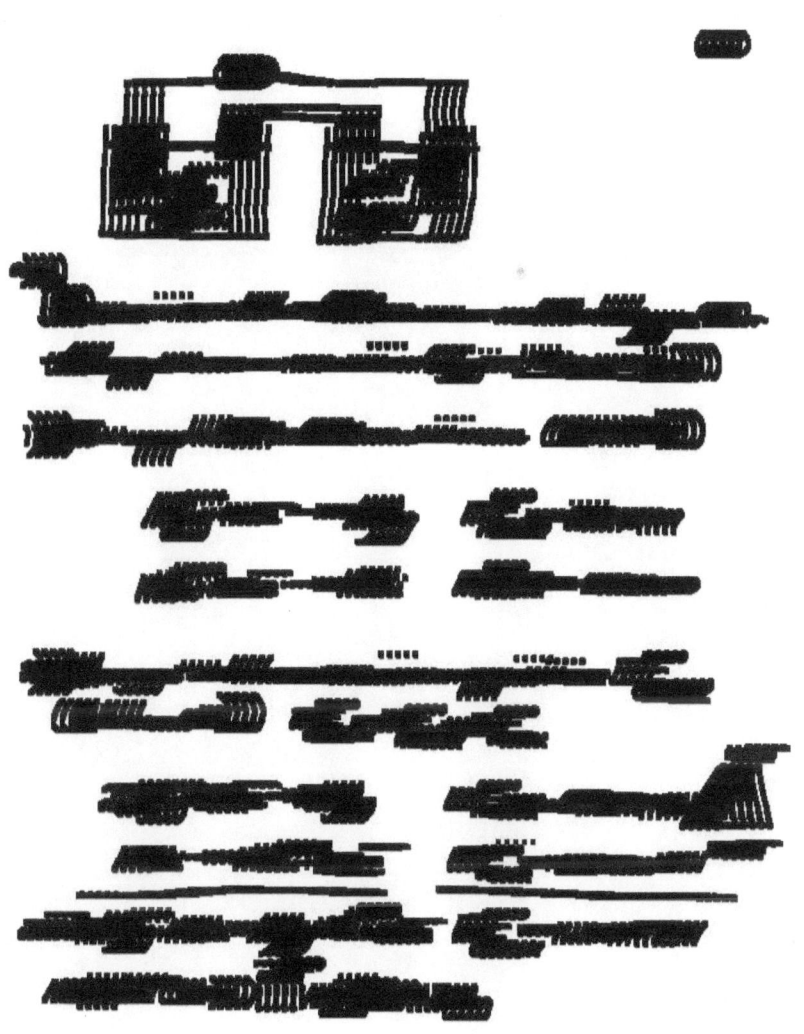

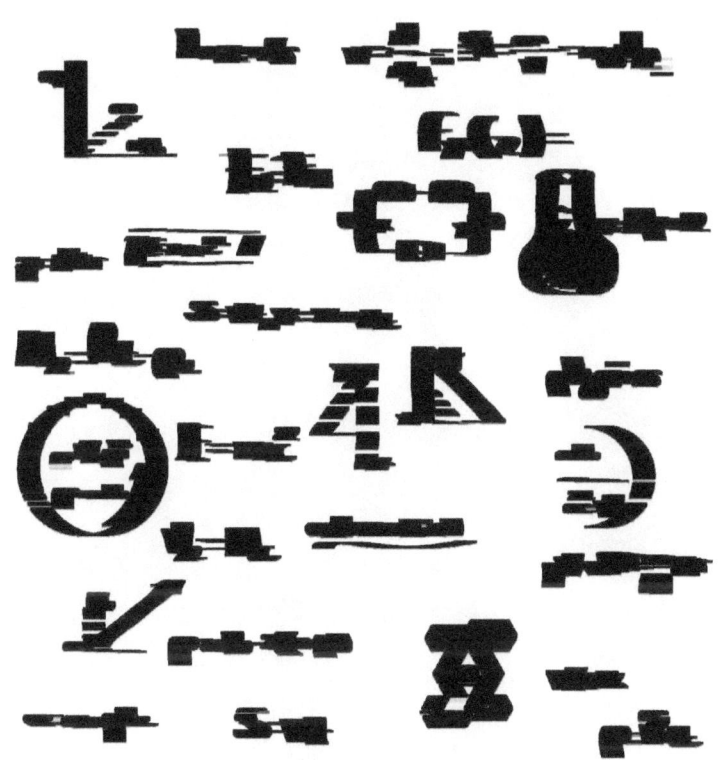

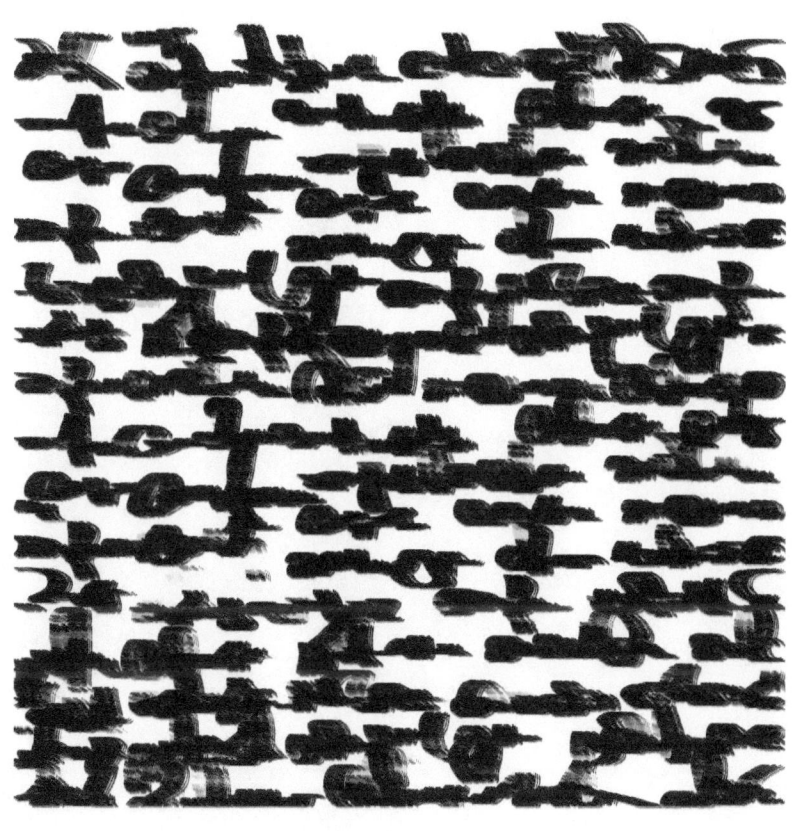

51

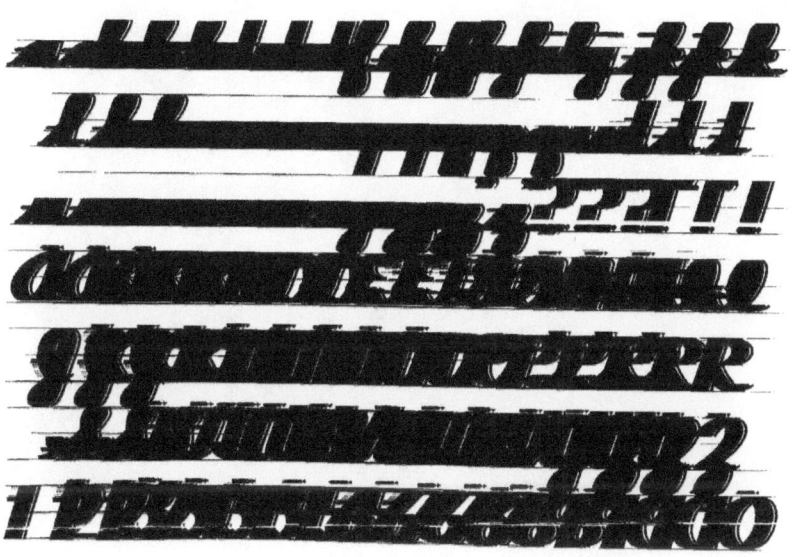

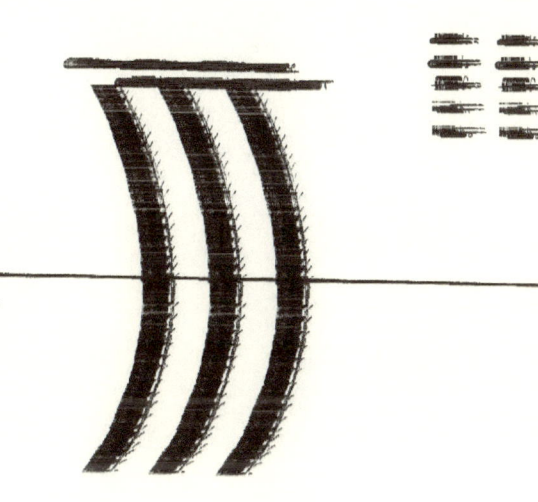

57

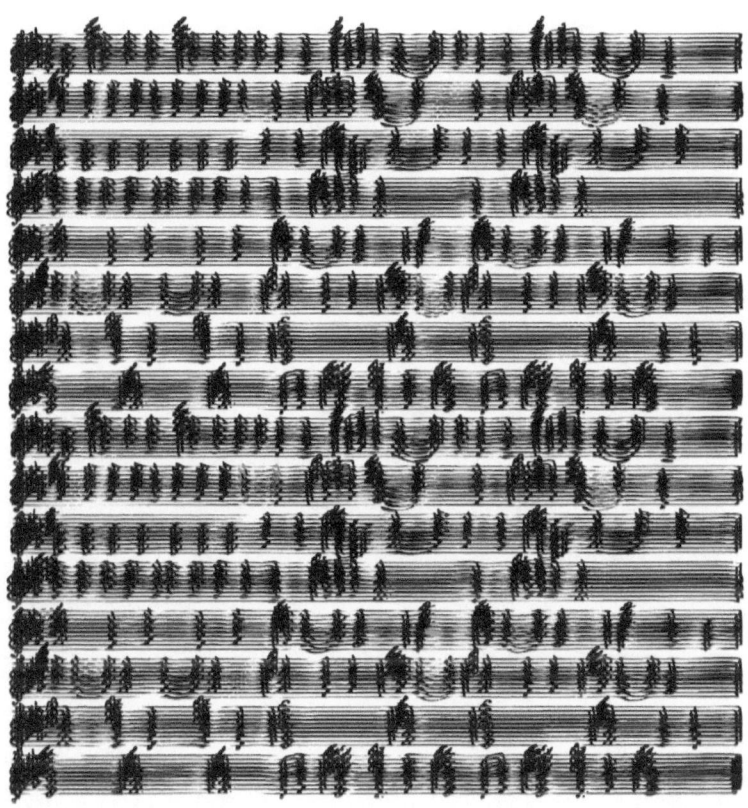